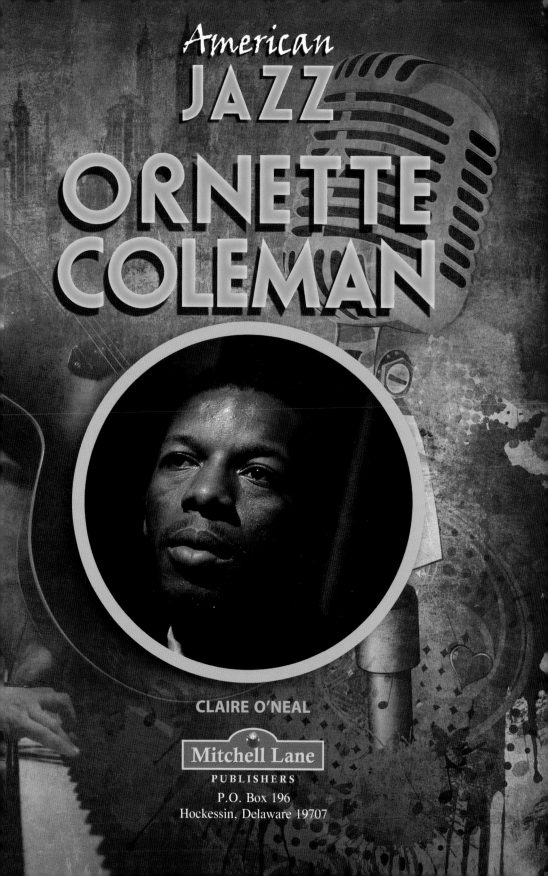

American
JAZZ

ORNETTE COLEMAN

CLAIRE O'NEAL

Mitchell Lane
PUBLISHERS

P.O. Box 196
Hockessin, Delaware 19707

American JAZZ

Benny Goodman

Bessie Smith

Billie Holiday

Charlie Parker

Count Basie

Dizzy Gillespie

Louis Armstrong

Miles Davis

Ornette Coleman

Scott Joplin

Copyright © 2013 by Mitchell Lane Publishers

PUBLISHER'S NOTE: The facts on which this book is based have been thoroughly researched. Documentation of such research can be found on page 44. While every possible effort has been made to ensure accuracy, the publisher will not assume liability for damages caused by inaccuracies in the data, and makes no warranty on the accuracy of the information contained herein.

Printing   1   2   3   4   5   6   7   8   9

**Library of Congress
Cataloging-in-Publication Data**

O'Neal, Claire.
 Ornette Coleman / by Claire O'Neal.
    pages cm. — (American jazz)
 Includes bibliographical references, discography, and index.
 ISBN 978-1-61228-268-8 (library bound)
 1. Coleman, Ornette. 2. Jazz musicians—United States—Biography. I. Title.
 ML419.C63O54 2013
 788.7'165092—dc23
 [B]
                                          2012019232
 eBook ISBN: 9781612283449
                                          PLB

Contents

Change of
the Century

It's a cold November night in 1959 on the streets of the East Village in New York City. That doesn't stop the crowds from packing the Five Spot, a tiny, seventy-five-seat club otherwise known as the hippest jazz joint in town.

Tonight on the bill—a new quartet from Los Angeles, fronted by Ornette Coleman. Coleman's new records have caused such a stir in the jazz world that *New York Times* music critic Martin Williams begged the Five Spot's owners, brothers Joe and Iggy Termini, to book the new act for a two-week gig. The line-up at the Five Spot was known to change frequently, whether it was because beat poet Allen Ginsberg was in town to read, or because Theolonious Monk's quartet happened to feel like jamming, or because it was time for the next big act to spend a little time at the top, having worked its way up through New York's other hot jazz clubs.[1]

And at such a time for the jazz scene! The year 1959 represented a changing of the jazz guard. New York's jazz world said goodbye to three well-loved legends in 1959—the soulful crooner Billie Holiday, her longtime friend and hipster saxophone player Lester Young, and master sax soloist Sidney Bechet. Through jazz, these innovative black performers broke down America's racial barriers. At jazz joints in the '40s and '50s, like Duke Ellington's Cotton Club or Café Society, white audiences from all over came to listen to Billie Holiday's mournful rendition of "Strange Fruit," a protest song that spoke honestly about lynching in the South. After kicking down that door, talented black jazzmen became the essence of cool. In 1959, bassist Charlie Mingus, sax legend John Coltrane, and trumpeter Miles Davis each released acclaimed bebop albums that would go on to become required knowledge on the hipster scene. These clean-cut jazz giants created an atmosphere of music as art, drawing crowds of white and black intellectuals—poets, authors, and painters—to their shows.

But tonight at the Five Spot, a careening, high-pitched, maybe even out-of-tune saxophone solo blasts out into the night, like shouting at a gospel revival. A trumpet worries in the background, dancing a two-step around the wandering bass and then soaring through a solo of its own. The drums can't even keep up. Or can they? What is this . . . this *noise*?

Inside, the audience is sometimes louder than the music.

"Fake!" someone shrieks.

"Genius!" cries another.

Front and center inside the hot, smoky, crowded club are three black men on stage in suits and ties, and a nerdy white guy plucking at his bass. The leader, Ornette Coleman, is a skinny guy with a rough beard and, wait . . . is his saxophone *white plastic*?

For many, jazz—especially live jazz—presents a unique opportunity to participate in the creation of something new. The hallmark of jazz is improvisation, where featured musicians create a melody on the spot. Improvisation can turn off listeners used to traditional rhythms and melodies. To them, modern jazz can sound more like noise than music. Ornette Coleman's lasting gift to jazz, first presented to New York at the Five Spot, was to revolutionize improvisation. Coleman saw pure, musical art in every solo. He created songs that used instrumental voices to express ideas and moods—more like paintings of sounds than traditional ideas of music. Coleman also insisted that all members of a jazz group should participate in this creative process, and not just the band leader. To some, Coleman's music is jazz at its weirdest—no rules, no structure, just sound. But over a more than fifty-year career of

Coleman and trumpeter Don Cherry debut their hot new sound with the Ornette Coleman Quartet at the Five Spot Café in New York City on November 17, 1959.

staying true to his principles, Coleman has accumulated more fans than detractors. He inspired musicians to reinvent the stodgy and sometimes snobby world of jazz by finding new sounds. Nearly everyone in modern jazz name-checks Coleman as an influence, from jazz giant John Coltrane to modern award-winning Ornette disciple John Zorn. Modern jazz aficionados enjoy Coleman's music as a conversation beyond language, challenged by his ever-changing pieces to live in the moment of music. Love him or hate him, critics agree—Ornette Coleman has forever changed the way audiences listen to jazz.

Ornette Coleman
performs on stage
with his saxophone

America's Music

The seeds of jazz were first sown in America's Deep South by African-American slaves. The rhythmic patterns of African languages gave a strong beat to working songs shared by the slaves to lighten their burdens. Africa's tribal sound, sung in a pentatonic scale, was played or sung slightly flat. This "blue" sound, now influenced by European classical music and church hymns, created the blues: a complex, emotional music that gave birth to jazz.

Jazz first gained popularity in black communities as music for good times in bad places. The earliest forms of jazz were created in "red-light" districts, places notorious for drinking and bad behavior. Scott Joplin's lively blues piano tunes with "ragged," syncopated rhythms became known as ragtime, tinkling out of the dirty bars of St. Louis, Missouri between 1890 and 1910. Joplin's sound made it downriver to New Orleans, where Jelly Roll Morton and others infused it with Creole and Spanish rhythms and sounds. The catchy, rollicking tunes made it to big cities like New York during the Jazz Age of the '20s and '30s, where masterful brass players,

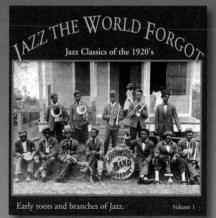

JAZZ THE WORLD FORGOT

Jazz Classics of the 1920's

Early roots and branches of Jazz.   Volume 1

like trumpeter Louis Armstrong, played big-band and swing sounds in speakeasy clubs. By the '40s and '50s, jazz was known as America's music. No longer just for black music lovers, white audiences, too, hummed along with orchestra master Duke Ellington, or followed the thought-provoking, arty bebop of saxophonist Charlie Parker. Now, enter Ornette Coleman, whose musical philosophy transcended both race and music to transform jazz into an experiential art form.

Chapter 2

Tomorrow is the Question

Randolph Denard Ornette Coleman was born on March 9, 1930, in Fort Worth, Texas. At the time, less than 10 percent of Fort Worth's population was black, and segregation restricted black families to the poorest neighborhoods in town.[1] Even back then, Coleman's neighborhood was on the wrong side of the tracks, and certainly he felt the sting of inequality in the racist south. But the Great Depression of the 1930s was an equalizer, bringing poverty, hunger, and joblessness to Americans of all races.

Ornette's family was lucky—both his parents were able to find work. His father, Randolph, worked as a cook, a mechanic, and any other job he could find to make ends meet. Ornette's mother, Rosa, worked from home as a seamstress. Though his parents were busy, they were kind, and Ornette and his older sister Truvenza remember being kids in a house filled with love. Music also filled the Coleman house daily, usually in simple ways like listening to the radio or singing hymns with their mother at church. Truvenza remembers that "my father sang. Not professionally, but I guess that's where we got it from."[2] Ornette's memories about his father are not as clear—Randolph died when Ornette was only seven years old. As a single mom during the Depression, Rosa was very strict, and though he tried his hardest to please her, Ornette also knew from an early age to stand up for what he believed in. He told *People* magazine, "One day a teacher spanked me because I told her she was wrong. I was hurt, because I knew I was right."[3] Frustrated at the injustice, Ornette stopped going to school for awhile. When Rosa found out that Ornette had skipped six weeks at once, he says she "beat me for days."[4]

Ornette first heard a saxophone in middle school, when local musician Sonny Strain brought his band to play for a school assembly. Excited, the young Coleman worked odd jobs, shining shoes and scraping paint around town, until he saved up enough to buy an alto saxophone with his own money when he was 14.[5] Without money for a proper teacher, Coleman taught himself to play by copying the sounds he heard on the family radio. But when he tried to learn music theory from a saxophone instruction book, he picked up a bad habit. Coleman mistakenly thought that the low C on his alto sax was the A-note printed in his instruction book's score.[6] It only made sense. That way, music notes followed the alphabet—ABCDEFG (instead of the standard, accepted naming of the notes—CDEFGAB). The result? Coleman's pitch was out of tune by a minor third. The first time he played a scale in public, during church band practice, the conductor ridiculed and embarrassed Coleman as an example of how *not* to play.[7] Though he later learned to play correctly, young Coleman's "mistake" proved serendipitous. It led him to discover pitch and harmony in unconventional ways, shaping the independent streak and unique musical theories that would define his career.

At sixteen, Coleman joined a Fort Worth bebop band led by young saxophonist "Red" Connors. Connors introduced Coleman to the music of renowned saxophonist Charlie Parker,[8] a revolutionary figure in jazz in the '40s. Parker, or "Bird," brought fast chord changes and new ideas about harmony to jazz, influencing nearly all jazz saxophonists since. More than his music, though, Bird was also a beloved icon in hipster culture. His status paved the way for serious jazz musicians to be seen as artists and not just entertainers. Coleman fell in love with Parker's bebop, a bouncy swing style of jazz where improvisation was king. He soon switched to Parker's tenor sax. Tenor sax was also a favorite instrument of the rhythm and blues tunes that Coleman and his mother tapped their feet to at home.

Coleman hoped to find work through his music to support his family. His mother helped him however she could, whether that meant letting Coleman's young instrumentalist friends meet at the Coleman house for after-school jam sessions,[9] or allowing the under-age Coleman to play for money at very grown-up venues. During the day, Coleman played in his high school band. At night, he played for money at juke joints, filling in for the usual adult players who were overseas fighting in World War II. But the seedy bars were rough places where people went to drink and gamble; the near-constant fights and police raids scared the teenage Ornette. He told his mother, "I don't want to play this music. It's making people kill each other." His mother gave Coleman a dose of reality. "What you mean," she asked, "You want somebody to pay you for your soul?"[10]

Coleman took his mother's words to heart—he knew he could not control other people's actions. He also was not playing the music in his soul, but he knew that he should be. He started playing the bebop that inspired him, but he was met with rejection and even anger from Fort Worth crowds. Audiences booed him off the stage when he refused to play the toe-tapping honky-tonk dance music they wanted to hear.

The echo of public rejection would become very familiar to Coleman over the next fifteen years. When the traveling musical act *Silas Green from New Orleans* came to town, nineteen-year-old Coleman saw it as a chance to break away from his hometown. *Silas Green* was a well-known black comedy and musical act that toured the South in the first half of the 20th

century. Coleman and his tenor sax played ragtime with *Silas Green* as they toured the South from Georgia to Oklahoma. But when he tried to infuse his improvised bebop into the lineup, he says, "they fired me for trying to make the band too modern."[11] Coleman refused to lose sight of who he was and what he wanted to do with his music. He found day jobs in New Orleans for a time, and sometimes gigs. He played short-lived shows where his band members hated his style so much that they stopped playing and walked off stage, leaving Coleman alone with an angry crowd. One night after a gig in Baton Rouge, a group of men took him out back, beat him until he was bloody, and destroyed his saxophone.[12] Racist southern audiences also did not take kindly to this strange-looking black man. From his "Jesus-beard" and straightened hair to his funky clothes, he looked absolutely unlike the typical image of the clean-cut, cool jazz musician.[13] Future collaborator Don Cherry recalls the first time he saw Coleman: "He had long hair and a beard; it was about 90 degrees, and he had on an overcoat. I was scared of him."[14] In Mississippi, the Natchez police didn't like the looks of the skinny horn-blower; they chased him out of town. But guitarist Pee Wee Crayton heard Coleman's sound and liked it. When he asked Coleman to follow his R&B band to Los Angeles, Coleman jumped at the chance to play for a friendly face.

Pee Wee Crayton

Minstrels

Part slapstick, part musical revue, *Silas Green from New Orleans* and other black minstrel shows played an important part in spreading black music to white audiences. The shows lured people in with comedy skits, but audiences stayed to listen to a phenomenal showcase of black musicians early in their careers. W.C. Handy, widely regarded as the father of blues music, traveled with *Mahara's Minstrels* from 1896 to 1903 as a cornetist. Bessie Smith, the "Empress of Blues," got her start dancing and belting out ragtime tunes with touring minstrel companies, including a stint with *Silas Green* in 1916.[15]

This is Our Music

Pee Wee Crayton had heard Coleman's talent and knew he could play the blues. But however badly he wanted work, Coleman refused to compromise his experimental bebop sound. Coleman recalls, "[Crayton] didn't understand what I was trying to do, and it got so that he was paying me not to play."[1] It wasn't long before Crayton kicked Coleman out. After all, how could the band make any money with Coleman's weird noises chasing the paying customers away?

Coleman stayed on in Los Angeles. His fearless style and playing caught the attention of Jayne Cortez, a beautiful young woman with a sophisticated ear for jazz. They married in 1954 and welcomed a son, Denardo, in 1956. Even though Coleman had to get a day job to support his family—as an elevator attendant at Bullock's department store—he relentlessly pursued music. He knew he was onto something radically new in the world of music. At the time, jazzmen improvised harmonically, creating sounds on the spot that were guided by chord changes set in the song. Coleman instead wanted to improvise the melody line, the recognizable part of the song. Coleman did not want to play music, as it had been written and practiced before, but to celebrate the voices of individual instruments working together to communicate ideas. The curious Coleman turned the Bullock's elevator into a study hall during his breaks, locking himself in at the top floor with a stack of music theory books. After two and a half years of working in elevators, the store manager replaced Coleman . . . with an automated elevator.[2]

Meanwhile, Coleman's gigs were few and far between. Critics laughed him off stage. If an audience can't recognize the melody, how could it even be a song? However, Coleman was finally meeting other jazzmen who appreciated his radical ideas on how music could be played. His new wife introduced him to a wider circle of musicians, including drummer Billy Higgins and Don Cherry, a trumpeter, both of whom were excited by Coleman's freeform style.

Coleman's unique sound also caught the ear of Red Mitchell, a respected and successful bebop bassist around Los Angeles. Mitchell was not such a fan of Coleman's playing, but thought his friend Lester Koenig, owner of the jazz label Contemporary Records, might like to buy the songs Coleman had written during his years in Los Angeles. Not only did Koenig want to buy the songs, but he wanted Coleman to perform them as well. Coleman put together a band and recorded his first LP, *Something Else!!!!,* in 1958. The album featured a standard bebop

quintet of himself on alto sax, trumpeter Don Cherry, bassist Don Payne, drummer Billy Higgins, and pianist Walter Norris.

The album crashed the cool jazz scene like a shriek of joy. Coleman's sax solos literally spoke like a human voice, carrying on a conversation through the music. Coleman flitted effortlessly, from a bebop sing-along to a blurred, swift riff to a honking, hooting shout-out. He did it all on a white plastic sax he bought simply because he liked the different sound it brought, more like a nasally voice than an instrument.

Coleman's wingman, Don Cherry, stayed with him in thought and deed, choosing to record and perform with a pocket trumpet, because it produced a tinnier, sharper, and weaker sound than its larger and

Ornette and his son
Denardo in 1969

more traditional counterpart.[5] Meanwhile, bassist Payne and drummer Higgins together teased audiences with rhythm. Higgins usually kept a steady beat, while the others would solo apart from it, eventually finding their way back. But Higgins had his moments of soloing, too, and in such tunes as "The Sphinx," Higgins' drum suddenly drops out altogether.[6] "Invisible" pokes fun at traditional musical structure, featuring a tonal center that hides from the listener.[7] The tune hinted that Coleman's ground-breaking group was ready to leave musical concepts like keys, chords, and even melodies behind. He told playful stories of personality in songs like "Jayne" and "Chippie," inspired by his wife and drummer Ed Blackwell's son.

Nothing on *Something Else!!!!* was completely new—heavy hitters in jazz like keyboardist Sun Ra and bassist Charlie Mingus had experimented with a looser type of jazz before, and modern classical music also used similar sounds.[8] But never before had anyone based entire songs, let alone a recording on such a loose, free, and human sound, in jazz music or elsewhere.

Following the recording of *Something Else!!!!*, bassist Charlie Haden, known for his beautiful and melodic solos, heard Coleman playing at a Los Angeles night club. Haden was taken by Coleman: "I'd never heard anything so brilliant . . . but almost as soon as he started to play, they asked him to stop."[4] Haden introduced Coleman, Cherry, and Higgins to jazz pianist Paul Bley, forming a band that lasted less than a month. Bley said, "You could tell whenever the band was playing, because the audience would be outside on the sidewalk, and then when the intermission came, they'd go into the club for a drink."[3] Although the group was short-lived, Haden joined Coleman, Cherry, and Higgins in a like-minded quartet that sought after a new kind of jazz.

Executives at the major label Atlantic Records took notice of Coleman's first album and signed him right away. He recorded furiously with Atlantic between 1959 and 1961, releasing nine albums with quartets. Though the band lineups changed here and there, most featured Coleman's long-lived association with trumpetist Don Cherry, bassist Charlie Haden, and drummers Billy Higgins or Ed Blackwell.

Coleman's album titles—*The Shape of Jazz to Come,* and *This Is Our Music,* to name a few—trumpeted boastfully about the changing sound he brought. The recordings cemented his music's ability to create detailed portraits out of sound. On "Lonely Woman," widely considered to be one of his best songs, Coleman's sax and Cherry's cornet call together in a minor tone to evoke the mood, with Coleman's solos creening a soaring lament over the strong, quiet drumming.

Recording suited Coleman's nature as a gifted and prolific melody writer. According to school chum Dewey Redman, "Ornette can write 10 tunes in 10 minutes."[9] Coleman told Nat Hentoff, "Tunes come very easy to me when I can see a meaning for the tune."[10] Coleman's drive to write came from his history of playing before an audience. Every time he played in public, Coleman always wrote a new program. "I thought this was my duty to an audience," he told the *Jazz Musician*, "I thought they wanted to hear something they'd never heard before." It wasn't until the early 1980s that he realized audiences loved hearing his old songs, too.[11]

The Ornette Coleman Quartet (L to R): Don Cherry (trumpet), Ed Blackwell (drums), Ornette Coleman (alto sax), and Charlie Haden (bass).

But the studio could not begin to do justice to Coleman's dedication to a life lived in the moment. Coleman's 1959 gig at the Five Spot brought his raw, unfiltered emotion to new audiences. Each night, the same songs sounded wild and different in the hands of Coleman and Cherry, where Coleman's carefully crafted melodies only served as a springboard for improvisations that ranged from quiet, passionate pleading to atonal shrieks. Quite literally, Coleman's own playing recalled the sound of a human voice. Drummer Shelly Manne, who recorded with Coleman, said that "he sounds like a person crying . . . or a person laughing."[12] He strives for notes that are sharp and nasally, and his tone can range from intense and emotional to light and gossipy. Using unique breathing techniques, Coleman forces sounds from his sax that range from a skittering chatter to a loud shout.

Coleman gave critics plenty to talk about. Two of jazz's most important critics, John Tynan and Nat Hentoff of *DownBeat* magazine, became instant Coleman fans. Tynan raved that Coleman "is showing more originality on his instrument than *any* of the group of newer instrumentalists on either coast or points between."[13] But Coleman's seemingly free-wheeling approach brought out impatience, and even anger in opponents. When is music without rules just, well, noise? Jazz critic Henry Pleasants laughed off the "singular noises he makes."[14] Trumpeter and critic's darling Miles Davis said, "Just listen to what he writes and how he plays. If you're talking psychologically, the man's all screwed up inside."[15] Some boldly claimed that, behind Coleman's new strategy of crazed improvisation hid a man who just couldn't play the saxophone very well. British critic Alun Morgan took issue with Coleman's self-taught playing methods, suggesting that "Coleman appears to be handicapped by his own bad fingering in places and frequently produces two simultaneous notes an octave apart."[16] *DownBeat* magazine critic John McDonough has accused Coleman of being an untalented hack for over thirty years, saying "jazz had never produced a music in which fakes could move so easily and undetected among real musicians."[17]

Jayne Cortez

Jayne Cortez and Coleman divorced in 1964. Cortez is now a celebrated poet and also a jazz musician with her own band, Jayne Cortez and the Firespitters. Cortez and Coleman's son, Denardo, has played drums for Coleman since 1966 (when he was ten years old), and currently serves as both his manager and producer.

Free Jazz

These claims rattled executives at Atlantic Records. They sent their new jazzman back to school, to the acclaimed School of Jazz in Lenox, Massachusetts. A new learning opportunity excited the ever-curious Coleman. His eagerness and open-mindedness found a receptive audience in his professors, who learned alike from him as he shared his new technique and theories. One professor deeply impressed with Coleman was the influential composer, musician, and jazz critic Gunther Schuller, who would go on to become one of Coleman's greatest advocates. Schuller noted Coleman's amazing gift of pure inspiration: "Perhaps the most outstanding element in Ornette's musical conception is an utter and complete freedom. His musical inspiration operates in a world uncluttered by conventional bar lines, conventional chord changes, and conventional ways of blowing or fingering a saxophone. Such practical 'limitations' did not even have to be overcome in his music; they somehow never existed for him."[1]

Coleman's contemporaries accused him of breaking the rules of music, when what Coleman was trying to show them was that music should have fewer, if any, rules. Most jazzmen knew the rule—you improvise within the harmony, respecting the musical key your bandmates are playing. Coleman's innovation was to improvise melodies outside of the harmony, creating a very loose and—critics would say—seemingly random structure. However, Coleman's tunes

Coleman (right) duets with Dewey Redman in the studio. The two met in their high school marching band and would later reconnect, recording together between 1968 and 1972.

are firmly grounded in jazz traditions. Drummers first lay down a pulling, swinging beat as a song's foundation, a nod to Coleman's roots in bebop and R&B. And though Coleman's freeform jazz seems to balk at being fenced in by chords, the playful Coleman and Cherry often step around each other in chords to keep a tonal center, at least for a time.

Prominent in Coleman's music is his yearning to create not *music,* as it had been written and practiced before, but to celebrate *sounds*. To the philosophical Coleman, *music* is a style—be it jazz, R&B, bebop, rock—with rules that limit what a player can do. He prefers to think of his compositions, rather, as *ideas* that use the sounds of an instrument to tell a story or share a mood.[2] His music considers the instrument and its player first. Why does a player choose an instrument? What kinds of sounds can that instrument contribute to a musical conversation? Coleman writes music that favors repetitive riffs, simple to key or blow for a particular instrument—the instrument's equivalent of a catchphrase.[3] He was one of the first jazzmen to use the body of his horn in song, tap-tapping on the metal or clicking the keys to make his point.[4] In a time when jazz represented the coolest of cool, Coleman's gentle, curious nature kept his jazz from seeming too arty, stuffy, or high-minded. Jazz critic Ben Ratliff said to NPR, "Jazz has this kind of shroud of seriousness around it and studiousness. And the general message of Ornette's music is that it's for anybody."[5] In many ways, Coleman's musical ideas are very American—curious, creative, and celebrating the power of an individual.

Free Jazz, released in 1961, represents everything that Coleman set out to accomplish. The LP is the very first recorded, album-length improvisation, with almost forty solid minutes of improvisation by Coleman's double quartet—two groups of four musicians—with one quartet recorded on the right channel (for the listener's right ear) and another quartet on the left (for the left ear). The album's name gave a name to Coleman's style, which spawned an entire jazz movement now known as avant-garde or free jazz. Instead of the traditional jazz arrangement that focuses on a melody or harmony with a little space for a solo or two, Free Jazz represented Coleman's songs at their purest —creating a mood where each member of the band can express themselves in the moment through their instrument. He encouraged each band member to think for himself, saying, "I would prefer it if musicians would play my tunes with different changes as they take a new chorus, so there'd be all the more variety in the performance."[6] Where sax legends Charlie Parker and John Coltrane had a band that backed them up, each member of Coleman's quartet played like an equal partner in a four-way conversation. The result is certainly not toe-tapping music, but rather the sound of thought, a fleeting experience created in that moment.

With the jazz world properly torn apart, Coleman never stopped in his pursuit of innovation. He took a two-year break from performing

Coleman plays the violin during the public debut of *Skies of America* in July 1971 at the Newport Jazz Festival in Rhode Island.

and recording in 1963 and 1964 to teach himself how to play trumpet and violin. In 1965, he reappeared and toured Europe with a trio—himself, David Izenzon on double bass, and Charles Moffett on drums. His tour brought the free jazz movement to appreciative overseas audiences, who were treated to the world's first glimpses of Coleman soloing on his newly learned instruments. He played in scratchy, furious rhythm on the violin, treating it more as a percussion instrument, turning the image of a violin player as delicate or restrained on its head. In Ornette's hands, the trumpet screamed and shouted, as he soloed with it in upper registers, ran it through smeared notes, and blasted strong accent notes.[7] Coleman shared these new sounds on one of his finest albums, *At the Golden Circle Stockholm,* recorded during his trio's performance in Sweden on December 3rd and 4th, 1965.

Mr. Neon Suit

Coleman's live performances are made even more lively by his eccentrically colorful suits, which range from purple velvet to multicolored, popping prints. Having learned at the knee of his mother, Coleman has designed and tailored his own clothes since his early gigs in New York. In the 1970s and 80s, his band, Prime Time, earned a reputation for performing in mismatched neon suits. The New York paper *Village Voice* devoted an article in 1987 to just his wardrobe.[8]

Chapter 5

The Shape of Jazz to Come

After only ten years on the nation's jazz scene, Coleman had cemented a place for himself in music history. But Coleman was never one to rest on his laurels. He was awarded a prestigious Guggenheim Fellowship in 1967—a career award presented for exceptional creative ability in the arts—the first time the award was ever presented for jazz composition. Coleman used his fellowship to compose his most ambitious work yet, *Skies of America,* a symphony written for a jazz quartet backed by a full orchestra. Coleman was not the first or the last jazz great to add jazz improvisation to a composed, symphonic background. Miles Davis, Gil Evans, Stan Getz, and Dizzy Gillespie, among others, wrote masterpieces of jazz and classical music, a style that jazz scholar and composer Gunther Schuller termed "third stream." But Coleman's work was certainly unique in that it featured periods of improvisation for each member of the full orchestra.

Coleman recorded *Skies of America* with the London Symphony Orchestra in 1972. Although it was originally intended for a quartet plus an orchestra, it was recorded with just the orchestra and himself, soloing on saxophone. On the album's liner notes, Coleman first gives name to his inner musical theory and philosophy, calling it "harmolodics." In harmolodics, Coleman seeks to tie together music with language, dance, and even the theories of time and relativity.[1] Music critics are quick to applaud Coleman's relentless pursuit of his ideals of

Coleman's quartet rehearses together in 1971. Left to right: Ed Blackwell (drums), Dewey Redman (tenor sax), Ornette Coleman (alto sax), and Charlie Haden (bass).

improvisation, but are slow to warm up to harmolodics as a new theory. Coleman suggests that harmolodics is really no secret. "In harmolodics, most people think that you just take a horn and play anything off the top of your head . . . Well, Western music wasn't designed to be played that way because no *one* instrument is designed to play all the music. But most Western instruments can play a unison melody,"[2] that is, to play *together,* with the same goals, in the same moment.

But what about music in other parts of the world? In 1973, Coleman traveled to Morocco to meet the Master Musicians of Joujouka, a small village in the Ahl Srif mountains. The Masters welcomed Coleman into their dirt-floor tent, where they played the oboe-like *raita* with him for hours in sessions of raw, primal intensity. Coleman said, "It's a human music. It's about life conditions, not about losing your woman and, you know, baby will you please come back . . . It's not that. It's a much deeper music . . . The musicians there I'd heard had cured a white fellow of cancer with their music. I believe it."[3] The Masters took Coleman to a sacred shrine, where he recorded "Music from the Cave." Coleman played trumpet, accompanied by the village violinists and lute-like *gimbri* players. The sessions would influence Coleman greatly, especially in the next jazz movement to come.

The 1970s was a tough time for jazz. Americans suffered through difficult times, juggling soaring gas prices, new and conflicting ideas about equal rights for women and blacks, and growing discontent over involvement in the Vietnam War. Rock music ruled the airwaves, its driving beats and simpler melodies giving voice to the frustration of a generation. Audiences sought comfort in rock's primal voice, in the wrenching lyrics of soul music, or in the good times promised by disco music. Audience patience grew thin with the intellectual and challenging nature of jazz.[4]

Perhaps inspired by Coleman's relentless pursuit of new sounds, jazz artists pursued a new movement known as jazz fusion. Vibraphonist Gary Burton and guitarist Larry Coryell released albums in the late 1960s that married elements of jazz with rock's electric guitar, bass, and keyboard. Fusion caught the jazz world by storm, in part because rock audiences lured to the jazz world brought much-needed sales of albums and concert tickets. Soon many prominent jazzmen, including trumpeter Miles Davis and pianist Herbie Hancock, recorded with their own fusion bands.

The possibilities of new electric voices excited Coleman. His fusion band, Prime Time, recorded *Dancing in Your Head* in 1976. Ornette Coleman and Prime Time took jazz fusion to a wild, almost modern-classical music level of performance with simultaneous improvisations within the group. Inspired by the full sound of a double quartet with two electric guitarists playing lead, Coleman rearranged the first movement of *Skies in America,* adding a funk flair to it as "Theme From

Coleman meets with Kurt Masur, music director of the New York Philharmonic. In 1997, New York City's Lincoln Center Festival dedicated their four-day event to Coleman's music. Masur's orchestra performed *Skies of America* alongside Coleman and his octet, Prime Time.

a Symphony." Coleman also treated audiences to a recording from his Moroccan sabbatical on "Midnight Sunrise." Prime Time attracted enough attention around New York City to be invited to perform on the popular late-night TV show *Saturday Night Live* in April 1979.

In the past thirty years, Ornette Coleman's recording career has slowed down, but he continues to write, perform, and teach. His award-winning live album, *Sound Grammar,* released in 2006, shows that he remains in fine, restless form. Though he presents songs from throughout his range of recordings, from "Turnaround," performed on his 1969 release, *Tomorrow is the Question!* to "Song X" from his 1985 album of the same name recorded with jazz guitarist Pat Metheny, this time he enriches his live solos with musical quotation, a familiar

Coleman rehearses in his lower Manhattan studio in 1985.

the ornette coleman trio at the "golden circle" stockholm volume one

BLUE NOTE

ORNEtte

THE QUARTET & PRIME TIME

IN ALL LANGUAGES

ORNETTE COLEMAN
THE ART OF THE IMPROVISERS

CONTAINS BON

technique in modern hip-hop music, grounding his own tune in the notes of familiar songs, from Rodgers and Hammerstein musicals to Igor Stravinsky's classical masterpiece "The Rite of Spring." *Sound Grammar* rose to Number Ten on the Billboard Jazz charts and brought glowing accolades that could only come to a man who had persistently pursued his own ideals for a lifetime. Jazz magazines and newspaper critics praised it with rave reviews, naming *Sound Grammar* as the best jazz album of the year in 2006. The album earned Coleman a 2007 Grammy nomination for Best Jazz Instrumental Performance.

The high status of Coleman's recent awards testifies to his now-universal reception as a true artist, and a musical philosopher. The French government commissioned Ornette Coleman to compose a piece in honor of the 200th anniversary of the French Revolution. Coleman's work, "The Country that Gave the Freedom Symbol to America," was performed in 1989. In 1994, Coleman received the MacArthur Foundation award, sometimes called the "genius" award, for his contributions to jazz music. In 2004, Coleman became the only jazz musician to ever receive the Dorothy and Lillian Gish Prize, one of the largest monetary awards given in the arts. The Grammys honored Coleman in 2007 with a Lifetime Achievement Award. His Pulitzer Prize in the same year, for *Sound Grammar,* was the first-ever such award given to a recording.[5] And in 2009, Coleman was recognized by the Miles Davis Award for his contributions to jazz, exactly fifty years after the legendary trumpeter voiced concerns about Coleman's sanity.

Despite the accolades, Coleman has never enjoyed commercial success, unlike some of his contemporaries and the many he has influenced. Perhaps this is because his ideas are so naturally radical. He caused the jazz world to question exactly what is music, in the process changing how we listen to jazz. That Coleman's vision has endured is a testimony to his genius, which comes just as much from his prolific and revolutionary ideas as it does from his determination to see them through. By staying true to his principles throughout his over fifty-year career, Coleman has won the respect of fans and critics alike, and shaped music for a whole new generation.

Dr. Coleman

On May 1, 2010, the University of Michigan bestowed an honorary Doctorate of Music on Ornette Coleman, saying, "Mr. Coleman, your performances and your path-breaking theories of jazz and music have transformed how musicians play and what listeners hear. Your self-taught musical education blossomed into a radically novel sound, giving the world musical styles it had never heard before. In your long career of ongoing creativity, you have played a vital role in preserving and enhancing America's cultural legacy, and you have cultivated the talent of the future."[6] President Barack Obama received an honorary Doctorate at the same ceremony.

1930	Born in Fort Worth, Texas, on March 9.
1944	Saves up his own money to buy his first alto saxophone.
1948	Graduates high school and joins traveling minstrel act *Silas Green from New Orleans.* Coleman is soon fired in Natchez, Mississippi.
1949	Tours with the Clarence Samuels Rhythm and Blues group. Quits when he is beaten by audience members after a gig in Baton Rouge, Louisiana.
1950	Joins Pee Wee Crayton and his band in Los Angeles. Crayton soon fires Coleman, who stays in L.A.
1954	Marries Jayne Cortez.
1956	On April 19 his son, Denardo Ornette, is born.
1958	On February 10 he records *Something Else!!!*
1959	Coleman works tirelessly in the studio, recording *Tomorrow is the Question* (in March) and *Change of the Century* (in October). He attends the Lenox School of Jazz in Massachusetts. In November, the Ornette Coleman Quintet debuts at the Five Spot in New York City, beginning a revolution in jazz. Coleman relocates permanently to New York City.
1960	Records *This is Our Music* (in August) and finishes *The Shape of Jazz To Come* (in July). On December 21, records his masterwork, *Free Jazz.*
1962	Retires from jazz, in part over money disputes with clubs and recording label, claiming that he is not paid as well as other artists. Teaches himself to play violin and trumpet through 1965.
1964	Jayne Cortez and Coleman divorce.
1965	Coleman tours Europe with a trio of bassist David Izenzon, drummer Charles Moffett, and himself on saxophone, violin, and trumpet.
1966	On *The Empty Foxhole,* Coleman debuts a new drummer—his ten-year-old son, Denardo.
1967	Awarded a Guggenheim Fellowship.
1972	In May, Coleman records his full-length improvisation symphony, *Skies of America,* with the London Symphony Orchestra.
1972	Coleman travels to Morocco to study and record with local musicians.
1975	Coleman forms a jazz fusion band, Prime Time, and records the critically acclaimed *Dancing In Your Head.*
1979	In April, Prime Time plays on *Saturday Night Live.*
1980s	Records genre-crossing albums like "Song X" with guitarist Pat Metheny and *Virgin Beauty* with Grateful Dead guitarist Jerry Garcia.
1990s	Denardo Coleman becomes his manager; together they create their own label, Harmolodic, carried by Polygram Records. Coleman works on soundtracks for the films *Naked Lunch* and *Philadelphia* and arranges a harmolodic ballet, *Architecture in Motion.*
1994	Awarded a MacArthur Foundation Fellowship.
1997	Inducted into the American Academy of Arts and Letters. New York City's Lincoln Center Festival is devoted to Coleman's music.
2001	Honored with the Praemium Imperiale Award by the Japanese government.
2004	Receives the Dorothy and Lillian Gish Prize, the only jazz musician to do so.
2007	*Sound Grammar* (2006) is nominated for a Grammy Award and wins a Pulitzer Prize.
2008	Inducted into the Nesuhi Ertegun Jazz Hall of Fame.
2009	Wins the Miles Davis Award.
2010	On May 1 he is awarded an Honorary Doctorate of Music degree by the University of Michigan.

Something Else!!!! (Contemporary, 1958)

Tomorrow Is the Question! (Contemporary, 1959)

The Shape of Jazz to Come (Atlantic, 1959)

Change of the Century (Atlantic, 1959)

This Is Our Music (Atlantic, 1960)

To Whom Keeps a Record (Atlantic, 1960)

Free Jazz (Atlantic, 1960)

Ornette! (Atlantic, 1961)

Ornette on Tenor (Atlantic, 1961)

The Art of the Improvisers (Atlantic, 1961)

Twins (Atlantic, 1961)

Town Hall (ESP, 1962)

Chappaqua Suite (Columbia, 1965)

Who's Crazy Vol. 1 & 2 (Jazz Atmosphere, 1965)

The Paris Concert (Magnetic, 1965)

Live at the Tivoli (Magnetic, 1965)

At the "Golden Circle" Stockholm Vol. 1 & 2 (Blue Note, 1965)

The Empty Foxhole (Blue Note, 1966)

The Unprecedented Music of Ornette Coleman (Lotus Passport, 1968)

Live in Milano (1968)

New York Is Now! (Blue Note, 1968)

Love Call (Blue Note, 1968)

Ornette at 12 (Impulse, 1968)

Crisis (Impulse, 1969)

Broken Shadows (Moon, 1969)

Man on the Moon Growing Up (Impulse, 1969)

Friends and Neighbors (Flying Dutchman, 1970)

Science Fiction (Columbia, 1971)

European Concert (Unique Jazz, 1971)

The Belgrade Concert (1971)

Skies of America (Columbia, 1972)

Ornette Coleman Broadcasts (J for Jazz, 1972)

Dancing in Your Head (A&M, 1973)

Body Meta (Artists House, 1976)

Soapsuds, Soapsuds (Artists House, 1977)

Of Human Feelings (Antilles, 1979)

Opening the Caravan of Dreams (Caravan of Dreams, 1983)

Virgin Beauty (Portrait, 1983)

Prime Design/Time Design (Caravan of Dreams, 1983)

Song X (Geffen, 1985)

In All Languages (Caravan of Dreams, 1987)

Live at Jazzbuehne Berlin (Repertoire, 1988)

Naked Lunch (Milan, 1991)

Sound Museum: Hidden Man (Harmolodic/Verve, 1994)

Sound Museum: Three Women (Harmolodic/Verve, 1994)

Tone Dialing (Harmolodic/Verve, 1995)

Colors (Harmolodic/Verve, 1996)

Sound Grammar (Sound Grammar, 2006)

Chapter 1 Change of the Century

1. Ashley Kahn, *JazzTimes,* "After Hours: New York's Jazz Joints Through the Ages," September 2006. http://jazztimes.com/ articles/17196-after-hours-new-york-s-jazz-joints-through-the-ages

Chapter 2   Tomorrow is the Question

1. John Litweiler, *Ornette Coleman: A Harmolodic Life* (New York: William Morrow and Company, Inc., 1992), p. 26.
2. Ibid., p. 22.
3. David Grogan, *People,* "Ornette Coleman," vol. 26, no. 15, October 13, 1986. http://www.people.com/people/archive/article/0,,20094758,00.html
4. Ibid.
5. John Litweiler, *Ornette Coleman: A Harmolodic Life* (New York: William Morrow and Company, Inc., 1992), p. 25.
6. Mark Rowland and Tony Scherman, eds., *The Jazz Musician: 15 Years of Interviews,* New York: St. Martin's Press, 1994), p. 31.
7. John Litweiler, *Ornette Coleman: A Harmolodic Life* (New York: William Morrow and Company, Inc., 1992), p. 26.
8. Ben Ratliff, *The Jazz Ear: Conversations Over Music* (New York: Henry Holt & Company, 2008), p. 63.
9. Dave Oliphant, *Jazz Mavericks of the Lone Star State* (Austin, TX: University of Texas Press, 2007), p. 124.
10. David Grogan, *People,* "Ornette Coleman" vol. 26, no. 15, October 13, 1986. http://www.people.com/people/archive/article/0,,20094758,00.html
11. Ibid.
12. Barry McRae, *Ornette Coleman* (London: Apollo Press Limited, 1988), p. 12.
13. David Ake, *Jazz Cultures* (Berkeley, CA: University of California Press, 2002), pp. 74-75.
14. Barry McRae, *Ornette Coleman* (London: Apollo Press Limited, 1988), p. 17.
15. Lynn Abbott and Doug Seroff, *Ragged But Right: Black Traveling Shows, "Coon Songs," and the Dark Pathway to Blues and Jazz* (Jackson, MS: University Press of Mississippi, 2007), p. 340.

Chapter 3 This is Our Music

1. Nat Hentoff (liner notes), on: Ornette Coleman, *Something Else!!!* (Los Angeles: Contemporary Records, 1991).
2. Barry McRae, *Ornette Coleman* (London: Apollo Press Limited, 1988), p. 16.
3. Alyn Shipton, *A New History of Jazz* (London: Continuum, 2001), p. 773.
4. Ibid., p. 779.
5. David Ake, *Jazz Cultures* (Berkeley, CA: University of California Press, 2002), p. 71.
6. Peter Niklas Wilson, *Ornette Coleman: His Life and Music* (Berkeley, CA: Berkeley Hills Books, 1999), p. 105.
7. Barry McRae, *Ornette Coleman* (London: Apollo Press Limited, 1988), p. 18.
8. Leslie Gourse, *Blowing on the Changes: The Art of the Jazz Horn Players* (New York: Franklin Watts, 1997), p. 124.

9. Alyn Shipton, *A New History of Jazz* (London: Continuum, 2001), p. 774.
10. Barry McRae, *Ornette Coleman* (London: Apollo Press Limited, 1988), p. 18.
11. Mark Rowland and Tony Scherman, eds., *The Jazz Musician: 15 Years of Interviews* (New York: St. Martin's Press, 1994), p. 34.
12. Chris Kelsey, "Free Jazz: A Subjective History," AllMusic.com, http://www.allmusic.com/explore/essay/free-jazz-a-subjective-history-t764
13. John Litweiler, *Ornette Coleman: A Harmolodic Life* (New York: William Morrow and Company, Inc., 1992), p. 60.
14. Barry McRae, *Ornette Coleman* (London: Apollo Press Limited, 1988), p. 21.
15. John Litweiler, *Ornette Coleman: A Harmolodic Life* (New York: William Morrow and Company, Inc., 1992), p. 82.
16. Barry McRae, *Ornette Coleman* (London: Apollo Press Limited, 1988), p. 21.
17. John McDonough, *DownBeat*, "Failed Experiment," January 1992, pp. 30-31.

Chapter 4 Free Jazz

1. Martin T. Williams, *Jazz in its Time* (New York: Oxford University Press, 1989), p. 216.
2. Ben Ratliff, *The Jazz Ear: Conversations Over Music* (New York: Henry Holt & Company, 2008), p. 59.
3. Mark Rowland and Tony Scherman, eds., *The Jazz Musician: 15 Years of Interviews* (New York: St. Martin's Press, 1994), p. 39.
4. Dirk Sutro, *Jazz for Dummies* (Hoboken, NJ: Wiley Publishing, Inc., 2006), p. 151.
5. Ashley Kahn, NPR, "Ornette Coleman: Decades of Jazz on the Edge," November 13, 2006, http://www.npr.org/templates/story/story.php?storyId=10551757
6. Alyn Shipton, *A New History of Jazz* (London: Continuum, 2001), p. 775.
7. Henry Martin and Keith Waters, *Jazz: The First 100 Years* (Independence, KY: Cengage Learning, 2005), p. 271.
8. John Litweiler, *Ornette Coleman: A Harmolodic Life* (New York: William Morrow and Company, Inc., 1992), p. 176.

Chapter 5 The Shape of Jazz to Come

1. Alyn Shipton, *A New History of Jazz* (London: Continuum, 2001), p. 775.
2. John Litweiler, *Ornette Coleman: A Harmolodic Life* (New York: William Morrow and Company, Inc., 1992), p. 149.
3. Ibid., pp. 152–153.
4. Leslie Gourse, *Blowing on the Changes: The Art of the Jazz Horn Players* (New York: Franklin Watts, 1997), p. 126.
5. Ben Ratliff, *The Jazz Ear: Conversations Over Music* (New York: Henry Holt & Company, 2008), p. 57.
6. Lee Mergner, *JazzTimes*, "Ornette Coleman Awarded Honorary Degree from University of Michigan," June 3, 2010. http://jazztimes.com/articles/26158-ornette-coleman-awarded-honorary-degree-from-university-of-michigan

BOOKS

Axelrod, Alan. *The Complete Idiot's Guide to Jazz.* New York: Macmillan Publishing, 1999.

Hughes, Langston. *The First Book of Jazz.* New York: Ecco, 1997.

Meyers, Walter Dean. *Jazz.* New York: Holiday House, 2008.

Monceaux, Morgan. *Jazz: My Music, My People.* New York: Knopf Books, 1994.

Szwed, John F. *Jazz 101: A Complete Guide to Learning and Loving Jazz.* New York: Hyperion, 2000.

Vigna, Giuseppe. *Jazz and its History.* Hauppage, NY: Barron's Educational Series, 1999.

WORKS CONSULTED

Abbott, Lynn, and Doug Seroff. *Ragged But Right: Black Traveling Shows, "Coon Songs," and the Dark Pathway to Blues and Jazz.* Jackson, MS: University Press of Mississippi, 2007.

Ake, David. *Jazz Cultures.* Berkeley, CA: University of California Press, 2002.

Bogater, Jillian. "Obama, five other leaders to get honorary degrees." *The University of Michigan Record,* March 22, 2010. http://ur.umich.edu/0910/Mar22_10/915-obama-five-other

Coleman, Ornette. *Something Else!!!!* Los Angeles: Contemporary Records, 1991.

Davis, Nia. "Ornette Coleman." *All That Jazz.* http://library.thinkquest.org/18602/history/new/ocoleman/colemanstart.html

Gourse, Leslie. *Blowing on the Changes: The Art of the Jazz Horn Players.* New York: Franklin Watts, 1997.

Grogan, David. "Ornette Coleman." *People,* October 13, 1986. http://www.people.com/people/archive/article/0,,20094758,00.html

Hentoff, Nat. *Something Else!!!!* (liner notes). Los Angeles: Contemporary Records, 1991.

Johnson, Martin. "Happy Birthday, Ornette Coleman!" *The Root,* March 9, 2010. http://www.theroot.com/views/happy-birthday-ornette-coleman?wpisrc=root_lightbox

Kahn, Ashley. "After Hours: New York's Jazz Joints Through the Ages." *JazzTimes,* September 2006. http://jazztimes.com/articles/17196-after-hours-new-york-s-jazz-joints-through-the-ages

Kahn, Ashley. "Ornette Coleman: Decades of Jazz on the Edge." NPR, November 13, 2006.

Kelsey, Chris. "Free Jazz: A Subjective History." AllMusic.com. http://www.allmusic.com/explore/essay/free-jazz-a-subjective-history-t764

Litweiler, John. *Ornette Coleman: A Harmolodic Life.* New York: William Morrow and Company, Inc., 1992.

Martin, Henry, and Keith Waters. *Jazz: The First 100 Years.* Independence, KY: Cengage Learning, 2005.

McDonough, John. "Failed Experiment." *DownBeat,* January 1992, pp. 30-31.

McRae, Barry. *Ornette Coleman.* London: Apollo Press Limited, 1988.

Mergner, Lee. "Ornette Coleman Awarded Honorary Degree from University of Michigan." *JazzTimes,* June 3, 2010. http://jazztimes.com/articles/26158-ornette-coleman-awarded-honorary-degree-from-university-of-michigan

Oliphant, Dave. *Jazz Mavericks of the Lone Star State.* Austin, TX: University of Texas Press, 2007.

"Ornette Coleman." *The New Grove Dictionary of Jazz.* Oxford University Press. http://www.pbs.org/jazz/biography/artist_id_coleman_ornette.htm

Ratliff, Ben. *The Jazz Ear: Conversations Over Music.* New York: Henry Holt & Company, 2008.

Rowland, Mark, and Tony Scherman, eds. *The Jazz Musician: 15 Years of Interviews.* New York: St. Martin's Press, 1994.

Shipton, Alyn. *A New History of Jazz.* London: Continuum, 2001.

Sutro, Dirk. *Jazz for Dummies.* Hoboken, NJ: Wiley Publishing, Inc., 2006.

Williams, Martin T. *Jazz in its Time.* New York: Oxford University Press, 1989.

Wilson, Peter Niklas. *Ornette Coleman: His Life and Music.* Berkeley, CA: Berkeley Hills Books, 1999.

ON THE INTERNET

PBS: Jazz Greats, "Ornette Coleman"
    http://pbskids.org/jazz/nowthen/coleman.html
JazzCast: Online Jazz Music from Lincoln Center
    http://www.jalc.org/jazzcast/index09.html
Smithsonian: The National Museum of American History, "Jazz Class"
    http://www.smithsonianjazz.org/index.php?option=com_content&view=article&id=65&Itemid=92
NEA: "Jazz in the Schools"
    http://www.neajazzintheschools.org/home.php?uv=s
Ornette Coleman: Official Website
    http://www.ornettecoleman.com/

arrangement (ah-RAYNJ-ment)—An adaptation of a musical composition that is different in some way from the original, such as for performance by a different instrument.

avant-garde (ah-vahnt GARD)—A group characterized by unusual, radical, daring, and especially artistic qualities.

bebop (BEE-bop)—Jazz form developed in the 1940s, emphasizing fast playing, unusual harmonies and rhythms, and improvisation by soloists.

chord (CORD)—Three or more musical notes played together.

double quartet (DUB-uhl kwar-TET)—Eight instrumentalists playing together to form two quartets. See quartet.

free jazz—A style of jazz, pioneered by Ornette Coleman, that encourages improvisation of all instrumentalists more than any specific harmony or melody.

harmony (HAR-mo-nee)—Combination of musical tones, especially to produce pleasing sounds.

improvisation (im-PROV-iz-AY-shun)—In jazz, the creation of music on the spot during a song.

jazz fusion (JAZZ FYOO-zhun)—A style of jazz that borrows rock music rhythms and electric instrumentation (such as keyboards and electric guitar and bass).

juke joint (JOOK JOYNT)—A nightclub where one can dance, eat, and drink. At the first juke joints, music came from an electronic music-playing machine, known as a jukebox.

lynching (LYNCH-ing)—Death by hanging, carried out by a mob.

melody (MELL-uh-dee)—The recognizable, singable tune of a song.

minstrel (MIN-strel)—A traveling show featuring comedy and musical acts.

quartet (kwar-TET)—A group of four musicians. A standard jazz quartet includes a horn (saxophone or trumpet), a bassist, a guitarist or pianist, and a drummer.

pentatonic (pen-ta-TAWN-ic)—A musical scale that has five tones in an octave, unlike a traditional European concert scale that uses eight tones.

pitch (PITCH)—The height or depth of musical tone.

segregation (seg-re-GAY-shun)—Separation by race.

third stream (thurd STREEM)—A musical style that borrows from jazz and classical forms.

tonal center (TOHN-al SEN-ter)—A pitch that grounds a chord or harmony.

About the Author

Claire O'Neal has written over two dozen books for Mitchell Lane. She holds degrees in English and Biology from Indiana University, and a Ph.D. in Chemistry from the University of Washington. Claire loves music of all kinds and enjoys singing and playing the piano (very badly). She lives in Delaware with her husband and sons, and shares a birthday with Ornette Coleman.